IMAGES
of America

ROBESON COUNTY

One of Robeson County's most important natural resources is the Lumber River, which received its name from the large lumber business that was conducted along its banks. The river is home to a large diversity of plants, including mountain laurel, azalea, swamp mallow, spider lily, and wisteria. Cypress, poplar, river birch, and water elm are found in the swamps adjacent to the river. Sarvis holly and Carolina bogmint, two rare plants, are native to the river.

IMAGES
of America

ROBESON COUNTY

K. Blake Tyner

ARCADIA
PUBLISHING

Published by Arcadia Publishing
Charleston, South Carolina

Library of Congress Catalog Card Number: 2003102693

For all general information contact Arcadia Publishing at:
Telephone 843-853-2070
Fax 843-853-0044
E-Mail sales@arcadiapublishing.com
For customer service and orders:
Toll-Free 1-888-313-2665

Visit us on the Internet at www.arcadiapublishing.com

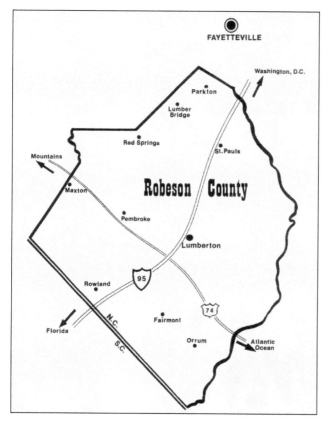

In the early days the Lumber River served as the main transportation route for Robeson until the county was crossed with railroad tracks. In the late 20th century Interstate 95 and U.S. Highway 74 have become the main corridors for travel in the county.

CONTENTS

ACKNOWLEDGMENTS

Robeson County has been a labor of love and a wonderful collaboration of the citizens of Robeson County. This project began as an independent study for my history major at the University of North Carolina at Pembroke. My wife, Bess, and I were able to find a large number of photographs in our own collection, the Hubbard-Tyner Collection, and this created a starting point for the gathering. I traveled the county renewing old friendships and creating new ones as I sought out the needed photographs and information to create this book.

I want to thank all of individuals who opened their private collections and shared their cherished photographs with me. They include Lyl MacLean Clinard, John and Betty Edens, Susan Caldwell Hall and Thomas Caldwell Hall, Mary Shaw Hughes and Carolyn Bethune Hughes, Patricia Knott, Jimmy Locklear, Hector MacLean, David Mann, Mutt McCoy, McKay Morgan, Flora Lou Morgan Morton, John and Dot Ray, Faye McRainey Reaves, Helen Seawell Sharpe, Victoria Smith, and Peggy Tyner Townsend.

A project like this would have been impossible with out numerous groups throughout Robeson County and the state. I would like to acknowledge gratefully the assistance from the African American Cultural Center, Border Belt Museum, Carolina Civic Center, Carolina Collection at UNC Chapel Hill, Centre Presbyterian Church Archives, Kate Biggs Collection at the Robeson County Public Library, Maxton Historical Society including the Mary McLean Poole Collection, McMurray McKellar Historical Museum including the Morrison Collection, National Archives and Records Administration, Red Springs Historical Commission, Sarah and Linwood Hayes (owners of TarPackers Restaurant), the Town of Fairmont, and the Town of Maxton.

Special thanks are in order for certain groups that have intensively supported this effort. They are Sarah Britt of Historic Robeson, Inc; Steve Massengill, supervisor of the Non-Textual Materials Unit of the North Carolina State Archives; and Lawrence Locklear, Bobby Ayers, Scott Bigelow, and Monnie Sanderson, the staff of the UNCP University Relations. Also, a big thank you goes to Stephen C. Edgerton for scanning and sharing many photographs from the McKay Family Photographic Collection.

The entire staff of Arcadia Publishing has been wonderful to work with, especially my editor, Laura New; she has kept my feet to fire throughout this process. At the University of North Carolina at Pembroke I must thank my boss, Art Department Chairman Janette Hopper, and History Department Chairman Dr. Robert Brown, who stepped forward to approve this project. My advisor, Dr. Stephen W. Berry II, has spent hours reviewing my selection of photographs and offering suggestions.

This book would not have been a possibility without one person, my wife. Bess has spent untold hours working with me on this publication. She has helped to look through hundreds of photographs and has read, reread and read once again every word of text. She has been a wonderful supporter of this project, as she has been of all of my projects. She has also had the added burden of our two-and-half-year-old son, McKay, as I have traveled around the county. She has been kept awake as I sat up until one in the morning typing away on the laptop. Bess, my darling, this book is dedicated to you for all of your love and support. Thank you!

INTRODUCTION

The history of Robeson County reaches farther back than its creation in 1787 and reflects the rich history of North Carolina. Carved out of the fertile farmlands on the border of North Carolina and South Carolina, Robeson County is North Carolina's largest county at 948 square miles. Indeed, it has been called "The State of Robeson" not only because of its size but also because of the fierce independence and self-reliance of its people. Robeson County is named for Col. Thomas Robeson, hero of the Revolutionary War's Battle of Elizabethtown and proponent for the creation of the county. Robeson County was literally a "Child of the Revolution" and was carved from Bladen County following the war. The residents of the area that was to become Robeson felt that their center of government needed to be closer and that the huge county of Bladen was simply too unwieldy. Even then, they sought the self-determination that is embodied in the spirit behind the county's nickname "State of Robeson."

The county is tri-racial, combining the rich heritage of the Native American Lumbee tribe (the largest Native American tribe east of the Mississippi), the African American community, and descendants of the white settlers, many of whom were Scottish. Situated in the verdant southeastern section of North Carolina, Robeson is bisected by Interstate 95, and is located near Fayetteville and Fort Bragg, the country's largest military installation.

This volume has brought together vintage photographs, postcards, drawings, and historical documents to allow the reader to take a trip back in time to experience Robeson County's proud heritage. Included in this volume are not only street and business scenes from long ago but also historical homes, churches, and most importantly, community life. The author searched extensively for images that formerly had never been seen outside of the families that held them. He gratefully acknowledges the overwhelming support of those interested in the preservation of Robeson County history in their generous assistance in sharing their images and stories. It has been a true joy to journey back into the past with those who also love Robeson County history.

This work will illustrate a major theme of Robeson County development, namely transportation. The railroad played a key role in this regard, and literally made its "mark on the map" through the names that many of our smaller towns and communities bear today. In the 1896 Branson directory there are 61 towns listed in the county. They ranged from Lumberton with a population of 1,200 to communities like Nye and Charm, each with 20 residents. While some of these areas are only a memory now, this book seeks to preserve those memories and perpetuate the study of their history. Today, the incorporated areas of Robeson County are Fairmont, Lumber Bridge, Lumberton, Marietta, Maxton, Orrum, Parkton, Pembroke, Proctorville, Red Springs, Rennert, Rowland, and St. Pauls. These areas still retain the small town flavor that makes them so pleasant to live in, as the images of everyday life contained in this book will show.

As you progress through this book you will notice many landmarks that local residents pass each day with no thought of their importance in the county's history. This work seeks to present these icons in a new light and to illustrate the true significance of each picture in the overall context of Robeson history. Special effort was taken to locate images that show these areas in a new light or an unusual portrayal in order to facilitate this vision.

The main purpose of this book, other than the preservation and dissemination of these images, is to spark interest in the study of Robeson County history and to encourage others to seek out documents, photos, maps, and other ephemera relating to the county history while it still exists. Every 20 years represents a change in generation and potentially a great loss of knowledge of history and its artifacts. If new generations of Robesonians are interested in their history and the study of their proud heritage, then the purpose of this book is fulfilled. Our future is truly rooted in our past, and preservation of this foundation is a sacred trust that we must uphold.

About the author

K. Blake Tyner, a native of Robeson County, is the Director of the Maxton Historical Society. One of his duties is the editing of the historical society's newsletter The New Scottish Chief. *From an early age he has loved the study of history and has a special affinity for Robeson County history and the stories of its citizens. Tyner is currently a history major at the University of North Carolina at Pembroke. He is also the author of several other works including "Goin for a Soldier," which won the North Carolina Society of Historian's Willie Parker Peace award in 2000. Tyner is a member of several academic honor societies and was recently elected FSA, Scot for his research into Scottish history in southeastern North Carolina. Tyner lives with his wife Bess in the oldest house in Maxton, Sycamore Grove Hall, where they are raising their son McKay.*

McNeill's Bridge spanning the Lumber River is a wonderful example of a trestle bridge. (Courtesy Historic Robeson, Inc.)

One

HOME LIFE AND FAMILY

For most people the thought of home and family conjures pleasant memories of running through fresh cut grass and sipping lemonade served by Grandmother. This is true if home was a small two-room plank home or a large ten-room plantation home. Home and family also means gathering for events like birthdays and reunions, or just visiting with cousins and neighbors on Sunday afternoon.

Archie Blue Tyner and Claudia Snipes were married in Bennettsville, South Carolina on August 29, 1929. In 1979 they celebrated their 50th wedding anniversary. They pose here with their great-grandchildren, from left to right, (standing in front) Joey Ratley; (seated) Lisa Ivey, Robert Thomas Clayton Jr., Claudia holding Ashley Clayton, Archie holding unidentified and Blake Tyner, James Benjamin Clark, and his twin sister Carol Lynn Clark. Grandson Russie Clark is seen peaking through the chairs.

When the early white settlers moved into the area now known as Robeson County, they were met by pine groves and swamps, such as those pictured here by the early-20th-century Lumberton female photographer Lillie A. Ferguson. This was taken near Ten Mile Church and School. (Courtesy of Historic Robeson, Inc.)

This WPA mural housed at the Red Springs post office shows the early Scottish settlers being greeted by the Robeson County Native Americans, the Lumbees. Early accounts state that this tribe spoke English and lived in plank and log-style homes. (Courtesy Hubbard-Tyner Collection.)

Often, large families lived in only a few rooms. African-American educator Charles Hunter writes of the home of Maxton railroad porter, Sam Crump, "I was puzzled as it consisted of only one room and a small shed room. In the living room were two beds, Mrs. Crump pulled a curtain around one of the beds to screen it and from under the other pulled a trundle bed." (Courtesy of Maxton Historical Society.)

Rev. D.F. Lowery, on the right, is shown on the porch of the Henry Berry Lowery Home. Originally built by his father, Allen Lowery, in the Hopewell area of Robeson County, the home was moved to the grounds of the Indian Cultural Center and restored. The center is the site of the annual *Strike at the Wind* performance, a drama that portrays the life of Henry Berry Lowery. (Courtesy of UNCP University Relations.)

The merchants and large farmers of the county wished to show their economic success by building larger and more elaborate homes. This two-story Victorian home with attached gazebo was built in St. Pauls by merchant and farmer Locke Shaw. Unfortunately many homes of this era have been lost. (Courtesy of Hubbard-Tyner Collection.)

William Stephen Cobb, son of John Wylie and Sarah Cornelia Owen Cobb, married Martha Harper on August 8, 1901. In 1908 he built a large colonial home on the outskirts of Lumber Bridge on the road leading to Parkton. A 1910 article talks of how advanced the house is with its electric lights, water works, and telephone. Cobb was elected senator in 1911 but died in 1912 at the age of 37. (Courtesy of Historic Robeson, Inc.)

William Jackson Currie, a Confederate veteran, built this 1876 Italianate cottage for his bride, Katherine Smith, daughter of Col. P.P. Smith of Walkula. Currie was serving as a town councilman in Shoe Heel when he suggested the town change its name to Mac's Town in honor of the Scottish who settled the area. They decided on a shortened version—Maxton. The home was named Sycamore Grave Hall by its current owners, Blake and Bess Tyner, and is the oldest home in Maxton. (Courtesy Hubbard-Tyner Collection.)

This Lumberton home, known as Riverwood, was built by Confederate Col. Alfred Rowland, namesake of the town of Rowland. His career as an attorney was put on hold while he served Robeson in the North Carolina House of Representatives. (Courtesy of Historic Robeson, Inc.)

Mill Prong House was built c. 1795 by Scottish settler and Revolutionary soldier John Gilchrist. Originally located in Robeson County, it became a part of Hoke County in 1911 when Hoke was created. Gilchrist served several terms in the House of Commons. His election win against Gen. John Willis led to Willis charging him as a Tory. Gilchrist was impeached and went through a difficult trial to win back not only his seat but also his good name. (Courtesy of Stephen Edgerton and Friends of Mill Prong.)

No family left a better example of their desire to build large homes than the Sellers family. Between 1791 and 1798 Archibald Sellers had 13 grants from the State of North Carolina totaling nearly 1,300 acres. He married Mary McMillan, daughter of Gilbert McMillan and Christian Taylor McMillan, and they were parents of six children. This home was built in the 1770s and was razed in the 1980s. (Courtesy McKay Morgan.)

This home was more than likely built for Gilbert Sellers and his wife Catherine McKay in the early 1830s, and it also served as home to their son William and his wife Julia Franklin Bethea. It was destroyed by fire in the 1980s. Both William and Julia had connections to Floral College, she as a student and he as a member of the board of directors. (Courtesy of McKay Morgan.)

RESIDENCE G.B.SELLERS. MAXTON, N.C,

Gilbert Sellers began construction of his Maxton home soon after his marriage to Flora McKay. The December 10, 1896 *Wilmington Star* reports, "Capt. Sellers has the lumber on his lot on Main Street, ready to begin in the erection of a dwelling as soon as weather will permit." He was Major of the Third Battalion of the Second Regiment of the State Guards and served in the North Carolina House of Representatives. (Courtesy of North Carolina State Archives.)

This wonderful February 1954 photograph shows the grandchildren of Wardell and Earmon Jones. The Joneses worked as sharecroppers on the Ashley Farm in the Philadelphus area of Robeson County. (Courtesy Patricia Knott.)

Early photographers often traveled through the county taking photographs of families. They would collect the money and mail the photographs to the family. Such was the case with the photograph below, taken at the Charles Upton Spivey home while he was away on business. From left to right are (seated) Francis Ivey Spivey (Charles's mother) and Amerette Prevatte Spivey (Charles's wife) holding an unidentified child; (standing) a family friend, Raymond Spivey, Warren Wirt Lewis with his ever present basset hound, Lillie Spivey Lewis, Lula Spivey, and James Spivey. (Courtesy Hubbard-Tyner Collection.)

Laura Kate Bethune (July 2, 1856–March 11, 1947) married John Calvin Shaw on February 11, 1886. She was the daughter of Duncan Bethune and Mary Graham McNair and great-granddaughter of Duncan MacNair, the first ruling elder of the St. Pauls Presbyterian Church. This tintype shows four of the children of the Shaws. (Courtesy of Mary Shaw Hughes.)

Expert canners, Mr. and Mrs. J.E. Bryan are shown below with their winter supply of canned fruits and vegetables. Canning fruits and vegetables was a part of everyday life and essential to feeding a family in the days before refrigeration and supermarkets. This photograph was taken by George W. Ackerman on May 20, 1932. During his almost 40-year career with the Department of Agriculture he took over 50,000 photographs. (Courtesy of National Archives and Records Administration.)

Confederate Veteran Gilbert Gilchrist McPherson, son of Alexander and Nancy Dallas McPherson and widower of Flora Sophia Johnson McPherson, celebrates his 80th birthday on August 8, 1904 with his family at the Philadelphus home of his son-in-law and daughter, James Franklin McKay and Ann McPherson. Pictured are as follows: 1. Samuel Rankin "Sam" McKay; 2. Mary Tiddy; 3. Jane "Janie" Humphrey; 4. Margaret Brown; 5. Annie Humphrey; 6. Catherine Tiddy; 7. Mary Jane McPherson Brown; 8. Kathryn Pearl Humphrey; 9. Gilbert Gilchrist "Gib" McPherson; 10. Sarah Tiddy; 11. Ann Flora McPherson McKay; 12. William "Willie" Humphrey; 13. William Davis "Willie" McKay; 14. Mack McArthur; 15. Archibald "Archie" McKay; 16. William Peter "Pete" McKay; 17. James Franklin McKay; 18. Catherine Jane "Kitty" Humphrey Buie; 19. William John David "Billy" Humphrey; 20. Harriett Sophia "Hattie" McKay Humphrey; 21. Nancy McPherson "Nannie" McKay; 22. Ella Currie McKay; 23. Margaret Nina McKay; 24. Carrie Brown Brown; 25. John Douglas Brown; 26. Mary Elizabeth "Mamie" McKay; 27. James Gilbert "Jim" McKay; 28. Florence Pate McKay; 29. Neill Brown "Bud" McArthur; 30. George Alexander McKay; 31. Katie Brown Tiddy; 32. William Edwin Tiddy; 33. Rosa F. McArthur; 34. John Murphey Brown; 35. Ann Eliza Buie; 36. Flora Buie McArthur; 37. Duncan Patrick "Dunk Pat" Buie; and 38. James Douglas "Doug" Buie. (Courtesy McKay Family Photograph Collection in the possession of S.C. Edgerton.)

On August 6, 1914, descendants of James and Janet McNatt gathered in Parkton. From left to right are (first row) Isabel Ray, Gillis Ray, David McInnis, Elizabeth Gillis, Virginia McNatt, and Leslie Gillis; (second row) Virginia McCormick, Nanette McNatt, Jack Johnson, unidentified, Rachel McNatt, Anita McNatt, Sarah McCormick, Sarah Currie, and Elizabeth McGeachy; (third row) John D. McCormick, Neill Gillis, unidentified, Sarah McGeachy holding Phillip McNatt, Neill McNatt, Clyde Gillis, and Alexander Gillis. (Courtesy of John and Dot Ray.)

Also attending the McNatt reunion, from left to right, are (first row) Anita McNatt, Neil McNatt, Phillip McNatt, Clyde Gillis, Alexander Gillis, Elizabeth Gillis, William Gillis, John D. McInnis, Neill Gillis, Sarah Currie, Sarah McCormick, Virginia McCormick, Elon Shaw, and Elizabeth McGeachy; (second row) Maude Gillis, Walter Make Gillis, Sally Johnson, Sally Brown, Flora McGeachy, Ann McGeachy, Nelia McNatt Livingston, Catherine Ann Gillis, Gillis Ray, Isabel Ray, Christian Johnson, Mary McNatt, Rachel McNatt, Adda McGeachy, Sarah McGeachy, Mabel Currie, Jack Johnson, Treva Johnson, Mary Pat Livingston, Sadie Hughes, Janet Livingston, and Mary Janet McNeill; (third row) Sarah Carolina McCormick, Ethel Johnson, John Johnson, Ella Gillis, Jim Gillis, James Johnson, Neill McNeill, Locke McInnis, John D. McCormick, John B. McCormick, Walter Johnson, Edna Johnson, James Johnson, Will Gillis, and Leslie Gillis; (fourth row) James Livingston, Dr. D.S. Currie, Dobbin McNatt, Virginia McNatt, James McNatt, McNatt Conoley, Don McCormick, Lauchlin McGeachy, Marshall Ray, Make Gillis, and John Gillis. (Courtesy John and Dot Ray.)

The McInnis family gathers for a Sunday afternoon drive. Seated in the front is John D. McInnis with his father Lock McInnis behind him. On the bumper are Catherine Ann McInnis and Isabelle Ray. (Courtesy John and Dot Ray.)

In 1914 extended family members gather around a car for a photograph. On the bumper are Allen Edens Ward and Homer B. Ward Jr. The front seat holds Letilla Edens and Bernard Edens, while Allen Edens and Lena Edens Ward are in the back seat. Standing behind the car are Edith Ward Edens and John Crawford. (Courtesy of John and Betty Edens.)

21

When fall rolls around each year people know that hog-killing time is soon at hand. In days before refrigeration, every smoke house in Robeson County would be loaded down with meat to last through winter. (Courtesy of Red Springs Historical Commission.)

Stills were once commonplace on many farms in the county. The making of moonshine was a family tradition and skill passed on from father to son. By 1916 North Carolina was officially a "dry" state. As we learned from the experience of Prohibition, this meant that moonshining and bootlegging became a large portion of the underground economy. The swamps of Robeson County served as a wonderful hiding place for stills. They were also found in barns and chicken coops or buried underground. (Courtesy of Historic Robeson, Inc.)

Two

WORK LIFE

Robeson County's businesses and work life have spanned all possible areas. Once known for its lumber and navel stores, the county advanced in agriculture with farms ranging from a few acres to several thousand. The introduction of the railroads crossing the county enabled farmers to move produce easily. The 1900 directory of Robeson County lists many of the types of business housed in the county. There were blacksmiths, cotton gins, cotton mills, cotton-stalk cutter manufacturer, flour mills, grist mills, planning mills, rice mills, saw mills, shingle mills, and turpentine distilleries. There were also many professionals practicing as dentists, druggists, lawyers, physicians, and a veterinary surgeon.

Sidney Hubbard is shown working on the metal lathe in his machine shop. (Courtesy of Hubbard-Tyner Collection.)

Lennon's Mill House was built *c.* 1800 for John Hawthorne Sr. The mill was later owned by the Warwick family before being purchased by the Lennons. The mill pond is one of the famous Carolina Bays and covers 1,500 acres. (Courtesy Historic Robeson, Inc.)

The mills of Robeson County have played an important role in the county's economy. Between the end of the Civil War and 1900 there were numerous gristmills in the county. Red Springs boasted eight mills, three of them being owned by women. (Courtesy Kate Biggs Collection.)

24

The swamps of Robeson County held large supplies of cypress trees. In 1884, engineer John McDuffie estimated that there was 150 million feet of mill-stock cypress left in the county. This 1890s photograph shows part of that cypress being harvested for shingles. (Courtesy North Carolina State Archives.)

Even in the early years of the 20th century, the woods of Robeson County still held large trees. This tree has just been cut by workers from the Seawell Saw Mill. One must wonder how they were able to move such large trees with only horses. (Courtesy Helen Seawell Sharpe.)

O.E. Seawell and his son Merton moved to St. Pauls from Moore County and immediately established several saw mills in the area. This mill even had its own small train; notice the railroad tracks running to the mill. (Courtesy Helen Seawell Sharpe.)

Joe McNeill moved to St. Pauls from Red Springs in 1911 and built a home on Blue Street. Across the street he operated a grist mill and blacksmith shop. It was said he could make everything from horse shoes to wagon wheels. The business closed in 1940. (Courtesy Susan Caldwell Hall.)

In 1908 photographer Lillian Ferguson caught these cotton pickers on film in the St. Pauls area, while resting in the middle of the day. (Courtesy Historic Robeson, Inc.)

The county's first cotton mill opened in Lumberton in 1900 and soon every large town had at least one cotton mill. The Red Springs Cotton Mill is shown with its looms running at full speed in the 1950s. The implementation of NAFTA has led to the closing of almost all of the county's cotton mills. (Courtesy Red Springs Historical Commission.)

Thomas Caldwell Hall gives McKay Tyner a ride on his grandfather Stamps Hall's restored 1940 Ford tractor. Stamps Hall not only ran his family's large farming interest on the outskirts of St. Pauls, but he also operated his own sawmill from the age of 15. (Courtesy Hubbard-Tyner Collection.)

The log barn stands among many on the Caldwell Plantation south of St. Pauls. This site has been in the family over 200 years and is now home to Susan Caldwell Hall and her son, Thomas Caldwell Hall. They strive to preserve this treasure left in their care. (Courtesy Hubbard-Tyner Collection.)

Jepthy Strickland (September 12, 1876–April 30, 1955), the son of Harris Strickland (1828–August 21, 1893) and Aneliza Lowry (1836–July 30, 1908), is shown in the fields of his St. Annah Church community farm. He first married Lenora Locklear (1875–December 27, 1932), daughter of James and Melvina Lowry Locklear. His second wife, Mattie Bell Jones (April 15, 1912–May 29, 1979), was the daughter of Rosezilie Locklear Jones and Daniel Brayboy. (Courtesy Lawrence Locklear.)

C.E. Morrison's Rowland High School agriculture class is shown estimating the yield of corn on the farm of J.W. Bethea in 1951. The yield was 80 bushels per acre. (Courtesy Morrison Collection, McMurray McKellar Historical Museum.)

The year 1978 marked 79 years of Fairmont's tobacco markets. At that time they boasted 24 modern warehouses and eight pack houses that were shipping a million pounds of tobacco a day. (Courtesy Boarder Belt Museum.)

Tobacco -- FAIRMONT -- Leads

BASED ON POPULATION - 3012- WORLD'S LARGEST FLUE-CURED TOBACCO MARKET

YEAR	POUNDS	MONEY	AVER.	YEAR	POUNDS	MONEY	AVER.
1919	6,998,393	$1,843,376.72	$26.34	1948	43,087,276	$22,797,709.85	$52.91
1920	6,956,339	1,834,386.59	26.37	1949	48,083,264	25,167,531.41	52.34
1921	6,499,599	900,194.46	13.85	1950	49,349,708	28,430,806.60	57.61
1922	3,511,795	798,588.18	22.74	1951	58,715,896	31,514,896.74	53.68
1923	7,869,872	1,803,774.66	22.92	1952	50,973,260	26,920,184.24	52.82
1924	5,008,010	891,425.78	17.80	1953	52,453,388	30,481,658.16	53.11
1925	10,254,363	1,875,522.99	18.29	1954	50,971,584	27,647,262.68	54.24
1926	9,461,431	2,409,826.48	25.47	1955	50,882,724	27,588,122.37	54.22
1927	15,766,672	3,652,586.23	21.79	1956	48,737,336	26,716,505.66	54.82
1928	18,736,422	2,819,831.51	15.05	1957	38,760,952	23,261,067.88	60.02
1929	25,367,668	4,439,341.90	17.50	1958	42,907,524	26,210,074.91	61.09
1930	33,429,431	4,650,033.85	13.91	1959	44,474,742	28,099,343.25	63.18
1931	28,757,968	3,298,538.93	11.47	1960	50,174,392	31,363,439.23	62.57
1932	17,268,844	2,139,609.77	12.39	1961	50,540,884	33,455,639.91	66.20
1933	32,911,040	4,498,939.17	13.67	1962	56,890,340	34,902,775.66	61.35
1934	23,661,874	5,846,375.32	24.70	1963	48,695,552	29,292,180.02	60.16
1935	34,006,544	7,201,329.54	21.18	1964	51,357,052	30,970,455.45	60.30
1936	29,893,592	7,042,960.03	23.56	1965	47,620,142	31,433,596.81	66.01
1937	41,036,038	9,525,147.51	23.22	1966	40,114,098	27,498,324.34	68.55
1938	34,825,280	8,074,742.75	23.18	1967	46,081,110	30,554,521.68	66.31
1939	45,825,232	7,214,522.84	15.74	1968	37,162,127	25,375,608.48	68.31
1940	30,174,210	4,968,423.60	16.47	1969	34,000,432	25,007,926.02	73.55
1941	26,689,472	7,195,561.00	26.96	1970	40,387,680	28,894,658.04	71.80
1942	34,061,706	13,220,749.84	38.81	1971	33,455,867	25,500,298.16	76.22
1943	28,258,403	11,312,564.72	40.03	1972	30,589,028	26,172,980.74	85.56
1944	38,138,512	16,621,731.04	43.58	1973	33,301,797	29,033,733.56	87.20
1945	42,252,874	18,734,924.33	44.34	1974	28,458,625	29,713,636.50	104.41
1946	51,957,870	26,648,771.08	51.29	1975	37,696,617	38,412,424.48	102.45
1947	47,855,698	20,922,967.92	43.72	1976	30,093,093	34,129,196.58	113.41
				1977	24,116,222	29,947,239.11	124.18
				1978	33,950,792	46,715,158.45	137.60

Fairmont in 1978 was the world's largest flue-cured tobacco market by population. In 1919 they sold 6,998,393 pounds of tobacco at an average price of $26.34 and by 1978 they sold 33,950,792 pounds at an average price of $137.60. The Depression hit the market hard; in 1931 the average price of tobacco was at $11.47. (Courtesy Boarder Belt Museum.)

30

Buyers and sellers line the rows of a Fairmont tobacco warehouse waiting the outcome of the day's auction. (Courtesy Town of Fairmont.)

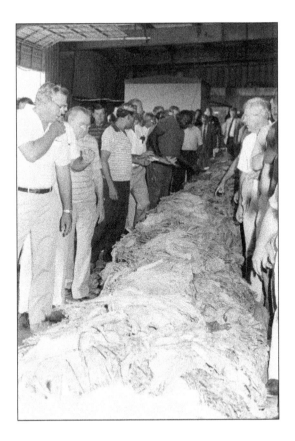

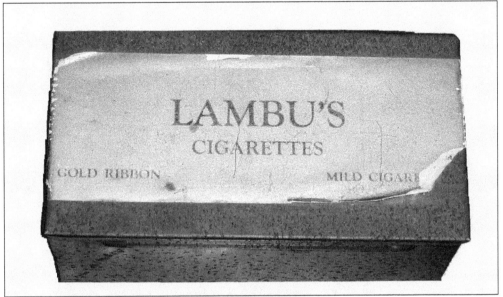

Lambu's Cigarettes were manufactured with 100% Turkish tobacco. This tobacco was experimentally grown on the Stuart Farm west of Fairmont from 1930 until 1934. Harry Lumbu, a native of Greece, cultivated the tobacco. (Courtesy Hubbard-Tyner Collection.)

The Wilmington, Charlotte, and Rutherfordton Railroad was the first to cross Robeson County. It had stops in communities that no longer exist, such as Bellamy and Alma. The Maxton station, shown here, was the last stop in Robeson County. (Courtesy Carolina Collection, UNC-Chapel Hill.)

In 1892 the Carolina Central Railroad was laid through what was to become Pembroke. The surrounding area was laid off into streets and lots by the Atlantic Land and Improvement Company. Pembroke was incorporated in 1895 and in 1909 became the home of the Indian Normal School, now the University of North Carolina at Pembroke. (Courtesy UNCP University Relations.)

The Maxton, Alma, and Southbound Railroad Company was incorporated on February 21, 1911. This railroad was largely an industrial line serving primarily the Alma Lumber Company. The line was abandoned on August 13, 1937. (Courtesy North Carolina State Archives.)

The Maxton, Alma, and Southbound Railroad Company extended its line southward until it reached Rowland, North Carolina. Here they constructed the wooden depot building shown above to serve this part of the county. (Courtesy Mutt McCoy.)

The Virginia & Carolina Southern Railroad came to the St. Pauls area in 1907 due to the work of Locke Shaw and his brother-in-law, Alexander R. McEachern, with Angus W. McLean. Shaw and McEachern owned the land surrounding the railroad; they divided the land into business lots that were sold by auction. This area soon became the business center of the community and the Town of St. Pauls was officially incorporated in 1909. (Courtesy North Carolina State Archives.)

The Virginia and Carolina Southern Railroad was incorporated in 1907. Angus Wilton McLean was president and general counsel while J.F.L. Armfield was vice-president and general manager. This photograph of one of Lumberton's depot shows workers taking time out to pose for a traveling photographer. (Courtesy Carolina Collection, UNC-Chapel Hill.)

The quote on the back of this photograph reads "taken Saturday our busy day." It was posed in front of merchant John Bethea Sellers's Maxton store. Sellers was born on September 9, 1866 and died September 9, 1925. He was the son of William A. Sellers and Julia Franklin Bethea. He, along with his brother Gilbert Bethea Sellers, operated the large Sellers family farm on the outskirts of Maxton along the Lumber River. (Courtesy Flora Lou Morgan Morton.)

When looking at this wonderful postcard of Main Street in McDonald you feel as though you have stepped into the old west. The town grew up on the lands of Richard Townsend. The post office opened in 1900 with James L. Townsend as postmaster. The town was officially incorporated in 1911 and in 1920 had a population of 120. This postcard was sent from Elrod on December 29, 1914. (Courtesy Mutt McCoy.)

This postcard shows Main Street in Red Springs. On the corner is The Carolina Bank and Trust Company. The bank's president was A.B. Pearsall, and also on the board were J.S. Jones, R.W. Livermore, George H. Hall, B.W. Townsend, A.T. McCallum, J.G. Williams, Dr. Luther McMillan, W.F. Williams, and Hiram Grantham. (Courtesy Carolina Collection, UNC-Chapel Hill.)

A.C. Melke erected the third brick building in Lumberton in 1866 to house the town's first department store. Before this, all stores had been called general stores. Melke's partners were Frank Gough and John Smith. The building later housed White and Gough, Inc. and then Rayless. It was one of the last downtown buildings demolished in the urban development. (Courtesy Historic Robeson, Inc.)

The wide streets of Rowland are lined with beautiful brick buildings. The town of Rowland grew up along the North and South Carolina state line and prospered because of businessmen like L.Z. Hedgepeth, William W. McCormick, Graham McKinnon, and especially Allen Edens. Edens was referred to as "one of the best businessmen Robeson County has produced" by Robert C. Lawrence in his 1939 *The State of Robeson*. (Courtesy John and Betty Edens.)

For time out of mind men have gathered in front of stores on benches to contemplate the problems of the world. Luke Blue, J.P. Brown, Wiley Taylor, Knox Kyle, Marvin Stubbs, Hyden Rouse, Royal Rouse, Nance Jones, and John Gibson are doing just that in front of the Pittman Drug Company in Fairmont. (Courtesy Town of Fairmont.)

In 1906 a large portion of downtown Red Springs was destroyed by a devastating fire. This scene shows Main Street looking north on February 18, 1906, the morning after. (Courtesy Red Springs Historical Museum.)

Before the advent of automobiles, the horse and wagon were an important part of every family. W.B. Brice and Son served the Fairmont area with all the latest in buggies, surreys, and wagons, as well as whips and buggy robes to keep out the cold. (Courtesy Town of Fairmont.)

This row of identical storefronts in Fairmont shows a large crowd gathered. More than likely this was a Saturday, when most people came into town to pick up needed supplies. Names of business owners—J.P. Brown, L.M. Thompson, and A.S. Thompson—are featured in stonework at the tops of the buildings. (Courtesy Town of Fairmont.)

This c. 1910 postcard was sent by a Lumberton resident who noted places of interest for the recipient. The resident points out the courthouse, Robeson County Superintendent Poole's office, the stores of K.M. Biggs and Townsend Brothers, as well as Dr. Rozier's Drug Store and the Waverly Hotel. (Courtesy Carolina Collection, UNC-Chapel Hill.)

The Bank of St. Pauls was organized by Dr. J.F. Nash, A.R. McEachern, and Locke Shaw in 1910 and was originally located in the building by the railroad that housed Ruffin Powers Store for years. This line drawing from one of the statements shows the 1911 building. The large wooden hotel that had been on the site was moved to the back of the block. After the bank's failure in 1935 it was purchased by the Bank of Rowland, and in 1943 it was sold again to Scottish Bank. In 1946 the bank left this building and it now houses TarPackers Restaurant. (Courtesy Sarah and Linwood Hayes of TarPackers Restaurant.)

J.C. Lentz (left) moved to St. Pauls from Raeford in 1911 and became vice-president and cashier of the Bank of St. Pauls. L.A. King (right) served as the bank's assistant cashier. This photograph, now in possession of TarPackers, was taken in 1928. (Courtesy Sarah and Linwood Hayes of TarPackers Restaurant.)

Notice the wide dirt street in Fairmont. The side of the Pittman Drug Store features a large display for Pepsi Cola painted under its staircase. (Courtesy Town of Fairmont.)

This 1920s photograph shows the line crew of Carolina Power and Light Company. Joseph B. Ivey, son of W.R. and Rebecca Edwards Ivey, is fourth from the left in the front row. (Courtesy David Mann.)

Red Springs was home to midwife Sara Ray. She is said to have delivered hundreds of babies during her lifetime. (Courtesy Red Springs Historical Museum.)

Miss Eliza McQueen of Maxton, a milliner, is shown wearing one of her elaborate designs. At one time no lady would be seen outside of her home without her hat and gloves. (Courtesy Maxton Historical Society.)

Mary Morrison Knight, also a Maxton milliner, shows off one of her designs. Another Maxton milliner was the former Lydia Pittman. Her first husband was Col. Francis Marion Wishart, leader of the militia during the Lowery Wars; her second husband, W.B. Harker, owned and edited the *Scottish Chief* for years. (Courtesy Bardell Collection, Maxton Historical Society.)

Robeson County is known for its ladies' clothing stores. This photograph of the Fashion Bar employees was featured in their Christmas advertising in *The Robesonian*. From left to right are (seated) Esther Lewis, Gerotha Cox, and owner Evelyn Price; (standing) Ann Thompson, Ethel Edwards, Ida Mae McNeill, Ellen Kinlaw, Mildred Kinlaw, Martha Baxley, Violet Lewis, Ester Mae Floyd, Lynda Nealy, Christine Thorndyke, Audrey McGill, and Laura Grantham. (Courtesy Hubbard-Tyner Collection.)

Malcolm Purcell McLean II, the fourth of eight children of Malcolm Purcell McLean and Almena Currie, was born in Maxton, North Carolina on November 14, 1913. In 1931 during the height of the Depression, he graduated from Maxton High School and with a second-hand truck went into the business of hauling dirt and farm products. This was the beginning of his transportation empire. He would go on to found McLean Trucking, Sea-Land Company, and Trailer Bridge. This self-made trucking magnate from North Carolina revolutionized ocean shipping when he took his idea—packing goods into locked containers—on a long postwar battle against the railroads, the unions, and the steamship establishment. The effect of containers on transportation has been likened in significance to the change from sail to steam. Rates, trip times, pilferage, and insurance rates all dropped. Profits soared. McLean is said to be the only person to have founded five public companies, three of them being listed on the New York Stock Exchange. *Forbes* magazine describes him as one of the few men to change the world. It is easy to see why Maxton's own native son—Malcolm McLean—is not only a transportation pioneer but the Man of the Century in shipping, as well. He is shown here with President Bill Clinton in the White House's Oval Office. (Courtesy Maxton Historical Society.)

Three

RELIGIOUS LIFE

Robeson County is dotted with churches, ranging from small wooden framed buildings with under 20 members to large brick houses of worship that boast hundreds. The denominations include Baptist, Presbyterian, A.M.E. Zion, Methodist, Church of Christ, Episcopal, Catholic, and the Jesus Christ of Latter Day Saints.

St. Pauls Presbyterian Church was founded in 1799, north of present-day St. Pauls. The Rev. Daniel Brown preached the first sermon and was the supply pastor for about one year. In 1848 the church moved to its current location on Old Stage Road using property given by Deacon Neill Crawford. The third church building was constructed in 1908 and used until the current building, pictured at right, was built in 1969.

St. George A.M.E. Church has served the African Americans of Maxton since right after the town's incorporation in 1874. It was the site of Charles Hunter's school in 1876. He spoke in his writings of the warm Christian fellowship enjoyed at the church during his three-year stay. (Courtesy Hubbard-Tyner Collection.)

Lumber Bridge Presbyterian Church was organized in a log building in 1793. Sherman's troops burned the church on March 11, 1865 and by 1868 the building on the right was built. The current church building, on the left, was dedicated in 1903, and in 1915 the church received reparations from the United States government for the burning during the Civil War. This photograph, entitled "Presbyterian Progress is Lumber Bridge," is by Lillian Ferguson. (Courtesy Historical Robeson, Inc.)

Rowland's Centenary Methodist Church was organized in August 1882 and the current building was erected in 1884 on land donated by Duncan A. McCormick. Three of Centenary's sons, Lacy Edens, Jack Ward Page Sr., and Madison Ward Maness, were called to serve the Lord as preachers. (Courtesy John and Betty Edens.)

The first time Centre Presbyterian Church is mentioned in the minutes of the Presbytery of Orange was October 4, 1797, when it called James Gillespie as its pastor. This church is located three miles north of Maxton and has served this part of the county for over 200 years. The current building was constructed in 1850, and part of the furnishings for the new building were bought on August 30, 1850 at James Mairs & Co. in New York. (Courtesy Carolina Collection, UNC-Chapel Hill.)

Harper's Ferry Church stands some three miles south of Pembroke. Set against a grove of trees within site of the rushing waters of the Lumber River, this nature scene brings you close to God as you worship. This was the site of the ferry operated by James Lowery, great-grandfather of Henry Berry Lowery. (Courtesy Hubbard-Tyner Collection.)

Antioch Presbyterian Church is located between Red Springs and Raeford on a hill that overlooks Highway 211. Organized in 1833, its foundation goes back to Raft Swamp Presbyterian Church, which was founded in 1770 and burned in 1827. The Gilchrist and McPhaul families played an important role in the churches' history. (Courtesy Hubbard-Tyner Collection.)

Rex Presbyterian Church was organized on May 25, 1913. Its beginnings stretch back to 1909 when the Lumber Bridge Presbyterian Church started a mission in the area. The Rev. J.E. Berryhill became the first pastor with a salary of $200 a month for preaching two Sabbath afternoons a month. (Courtesy Hubbard-Tyner Collection.)

The Chestnut Methodist Church is located on Chestnut Street in downtown Lumberton. It is thought to have been the church that Bishop Asbury was referring to in 1803 when he said, "Unlike many other places, families of respectability and influence were joining the church." (Courtesy Historical Robeson, Inc.)

The Burnt Swamp Baptist Church was organized in 1877 in the Jamestown Community east of Pembroke. The old church building was relocated to the grounds of the Burnt Swamp Baptist Association in the 1980s. (Courtesy Hubbard-Tyner Collection.)

The Burnt Swamp Baptist Association broke ground for the building on October 14, 1973. Dr. English Jones served as the chairman of the building committee. The association has supported the Odum Children's Home for years. (Courtesy Hubbard-Tyner Collection.)

Philadelphus Presbyterian Church was organized sometime between 1797 and 1799 with Rev. Daniel Brown as its first pastor. The caption on the back of this photograph reads, "The Garden Spot of the Earth." (Courtesy Peggy Tyner Townsend.)

Baptist Parsonage, Fairmont, N. C.

This postcard of the Baptist Parsonage in Fairmont was sent by a boarder staying there in 1912. He marked the room in which he was staying with an "X." (Courtesy North Carolina State Archives.)

Ashpole Church is located on the outskirts of Rowland. This first church was built on land donated by Othneil Traywick on January 2, 1796. The current building was constructed shortly before the Civil War. The name Ashpole was said to have come from the John Cade's bridges. Cade built his two bridges across the swamp out of Ash tree poles. (Courtesy Hubbard-Tyner Collection.)

Four

EDUCATION

Education has always played an important role in Robeson County. From one-room schools that held all grades to large multi-room wooden and brick buildings, Robeson County has been dotted with private academies and public schools. In the late 1980s all of the public schools in the county merged to form the Public Schools of Robeson County. Over the years six colleges have called Robeson home. Remaining now are Robeson County Community College and the University of North Carolina at Pembroke. The county was also blessed to have been home to 13 Rosenwald schools, funded in part by Julius Rosenwald, chairman of Sears Roebuck.

The student body of Barker Ten Mile School poses in front of their building. (Courtesy of Jimmy Howell.)

R.D. Caldwell, Berry Godwin, Frank Gough, A.C. Melke, and E.K. Proctor Jr. founded the Robeson Institute in Lumberton in 1891. Operated until 1907, the school was led by John Duckett, former superintendent of Public Instruction of Wake County, and Gen. Thomas F. Toon. The school's motto was "Do Right." (Courtesy of Carolina Collection, UNC-Chapel Hill.)

The residents of Lumber Bridge built this wonderful brick school in 1905. Hundreds of students were educated within its walls over the years. (Courtesy of Historic Robeson, Inc.)

The Philadelphus graduating class of 1911 takes time to pose for a photograph. Sitting are Mack McArthur (left) and Ruby Terry (right). Standing are Edwin Stewart, Lois Johnson, Sarah Smith, Ella McKay, Isabelle McKenzie, and Evan Norwood. (Courtesy of McKay Family Photograph Collection in the possession of S.C. Edgerton.)

In 1907 the students of the Philadelphus School sit for a photograph. Notice the beautiful building that housed them. It was destroyed years ago. (Courtesy of McKay Family Photograph Collection in the possession of S.C. Edgerton.)

First meeting of the Board of Trustees of Parkton Graded School District.

Office of Bank of Parkton, Parkton, N.C. May 23, 1911.

Pursuant to an Act of the General Assembly of North Carolina, ratified on March 4, 1911, which Act was ratified by an election held on the first Monday in May 1911, J.S. Hughes, Collier Cobb, O.L. Johnson, J.B. McCormick, W.L. Stanton, and A.H. Perry, constituting the Board of Trustees of the Parkton Graded School District, to facilitate and complete the organization of said Board

This ledger page shows the minutes of the first meeting of the Parkton School Board. For years they ran a wonderful school system before it merged with the county system. (Courtesy of Mary Shaw Hughes.)

This is the 1931 first grade at Fairmont. From left to right are (first row) Sarah Small, Letha Curry, Hazel Lovill, Mary Nancy, Odessie ?, Hilda Atkinson, Lucille Jenkins, Ima Jean McCormick, and Annie Lee Britt; (second row) Carson Prevatt, Chivian Currin, Alice Townsend, unknown, Allen Gibson, Wilber Willoughby, and Myrtle Britt; (third row) Ernest Klander, F.L., Byron Fields, Barns Lovill, Walter Sellers, and Jennings Walters. (Courtesy of Hubbard-Tyner Collection.)

56

This one-room Native American schoolhouse was moved to the ground of the Robeson County Planetarium and restored in 1971. (Courtesy of Hubbard-Tyner Collection.)

The Rosenwald schools were funded in part by a foundation established by Julius Rosenwald, who built Sears Roebuck into the America's leading mail-order house. The foundation did not pay the entire costs of the schools but required that communities help, and these schools were often called the schools that "pennies and nickels built." This school started as the Robeson County Training school but was renamed after its long-time leader, Robert B. Dean. (Courtesy of North Carolina State Archives.)

The St. Pauls Rosenwald School served as a legacy to Rosenwald, whose commitment to social justice lead to historic changes for black Americans. Although this school has long since been torn down, the site now holds the St. Pauls Elementary School. (Courtesy of North Carolina State Archives.)

Joseph K. Hart, in his article "The Negro Builds for Himself," talks of the people of Lumber Bridge who gave 70,000 feet of lumber for framing and sheathing. This lumber was cut from their lands, milled, and hauled by their own teams to a school lot purchased with their own funds. (Courtesy of North Carolina State Archives.)

Charles Hunter was born a slave in 1851, and with the help and support of his owners, he and his brother both became educators. Hunter's first teaching job was in 1876 in Shoe Heel (currently Maxton). In his 1928 booklet "Review of Negro Life in North Carolina with My Recollections," he chronicles not only his trip to Shoe Heel but also his life in the newly incorporated town and his pupils. (Courtesy of North Carolina State Archives.)

Maxton carried on the in tradition started by Charles Hunter by providing education opportunities for the area's African Americans. (Courtesy of Peggy Tyner Townsend.)

In 1841, John Gilchrist Jr. and others felt that the educational needs of the young ladies of the Robeson County area were not being filled. Their answer was the founding of Floral College, the first female college in the state to confer degrees. John, the first UNC graduate from Robeson County, knew the importance of a sound education. A student did this painting of the college. (Courtesy of Centre Presbyterian Church Archives.)

The graduates of Floral College held a reunion on May 27, 1934 at Flora McDonald College. From left to right are (sitting) Ida Carmichael McQueen, Cornelia McCallum Purcell, Mary B. Smith McLean, Flora McNeill Johnson, Nannie Buie Monroe, Kate McMillan Denny, and Hattie McBryde; (standing) Fannie Townsend Covington, Ella McIntyre, Serena Corbett Moore (daughter of graduate Mary Ann Stevens), Sallie Sinclair, Lou McCallum Fulmore, Janie McCallum Hamer, Janie Graham Russ, Cora McCormac Rogers, Flora Buchanan, and Louanna Purcell McMillan. (Courtesy of Centre Presbyterian Church Archives.)

Floral College was closed in 1872 and reopened as a public school. Some of the students gather on the front lawn in the image above. (Courtesy of Centre Presbyterian Church Archives.)

Rev. H.G. Hill purchased Stewart Hall, the former dorm of Floral College, and used it as his residence for several years. In 1950 the building was moved just down the road to the site of Centre Church and is used for classrooms and a library. (Courtesy Centre Presbyterian Church Archives.)

Prof. Marcellus Wooten moved the North Carolina Military Academy from Fayetteville to Red Springs in 1899. This photograph of the band was taken about the time of the move. The academy flourished until 1908. Students who attended the academy included Dr. H.H. Hodgin, Chesley McCaskill, and Tom DeVane. (Courtesy of North Carolina State Archives.)

The football team of the North Carolina Military Academy looks like they are not only ready to play during the 1899 season but also to win! (Courtesy of North Carolina State Archives.)

A movement in North Carolina for the higher education of women led to the founding of Flora MacDonald College in 1896. The Fayetteville Presbytery decided to establish a seminary for girls somewhere in the area. Red Springs came forward with the promise of $2,500, four acres of land, and 40 students, if the school should be located there. The offer was immediately accepted. This photograph was taken before 1919 when the trademark dome was added. (Courtesy Carolina Collection, UNC-Chapel Hill.)

Dr. Charles G. Vardell originally started the gardens of Flora McDonald College. Under his guidance and that of his capable assistant, Dexter Garner, the gardens became nationally known. Considerable damage was done by a 1984 tornado and restoration has brought them back to a point where one can still walk the meandering paths, and many of the original plants gathered by Dr. Vardell survive. (Courtesy of Carolina Collection, UNC-Chapel Hill.)

The cornerstone for Carolina Methodist College for Women was laid in 1908 but construction was not finished until 1912. Opening enrollment was 65 girls from Georgia and the Carolinas. Reverend Mercer served as first president, followed by Reverend R.B. John, and finally S.E. Green. In 1926 Trinity College (now Duke University) received the Duke legacy with the condition that they accept women. The Methodist now saw no need for continuing Carolina College and it was voted to close the campus. (Courtesy Mary McLean Poole Collection, Maxton Historical Society.)

The Fayetteville Presbyterian acquired the former Carolina College property from the Methodist Conference for $35,000 and established the Presbyterian Junior College. This photograph was taken soon after its opening in September 1929. In 1961 it merged with Flora McDonald College to form St. Andrews Presbyterian College and moved to Laurinburg. The old campus housed the Carolina Military Academy for the next 10 years. The main building of the campus burned in 1973. (Courtesy of McKay Family Photograph Collection in the possession of S.C. Edgerton.)

On March 7, 1887 the General
Assembly of North Carolina enacted
legislation, sponsored by Rep. Hamilton
McMillan of Robeson County, creating
the Croatan Normal School. The
school was founded to train Native
American public school teachers. For
many years, the instruction was at the
elementary and secondary level, and
the first diploma was awarded in 1905.
Rev. W.L. Moore served as the first
principal of the school. (Courtesy of
UNCP University Relations.)

TAKE NOTICE !

A Call to the Indians of Robeson and Adjoining Counties.

The men, women and children of the Indian race
are specially requested to assemble at
the New College Building at

Pembroke, N.C., Saturday, November 13th, 1909,

AT 11 O'CLOCK A. M.

Educational addresses will be delivered by selected speakers.
Music will be furnished by the Indian Band. Come one and
all and help us raise the money to pay the indebtedness on
said building.

All subscriptions are due this day.

Board Trustees Croatan Normal School,

A. N. LOCKLEAR,   O. R. SAMPSON,
        Secretary.   Chairman.

This flyer was issued by O.R.
Sampson and A.N. Locklear,
members of the Board of Trustees
of the Croatan Normal School,
inviting all "Indians of Robeson
and Adjoining Counties" to
attend the November 13, 1909
open house of the new college
building. (Courtesy of North
Carolina State Archives.)

65

This photograph was taken shortly after Old Main was built in 1923. In 1926, the board of trustees added a two-year normal program beyond high school and phased out elementary instruction. The first 10 diplomas were awarded in 1928, when the state accredited the school as a "standard normal school." Additional college classes were offered beginning in 1931, and in 1939 a fourth year was added with the first degrees conferred in 1940. (Courtesy of UNCP University Relations.)

The building now known as Old Main caught fire March 18, 1973. Plans were put into action to raze the building and build a new performing arts center in its place. A group of concerned citizens formed a group called Save Old Main and convinced the college's leadership to restore the building. It now houses the Native American Museum. (Courtesy of UNCP University Relations.)

Five

GOVERNMENT

Robeson County has been blessed to have been governed by a long line of proud men and women, starting with its first Clerk of Court of Pleas and Quarter Sessions Josiah Barnes and Sheriff Samuel Porter, until the current Sheriff Glenn Maynor and Clerk of Court Jo Ann Locklear. We have been represented in Raleigh by Robesonians like Hector MacLean, Robert Parnell, John Gilchrist, John Hasty, Ronnie Sutton, and David Bonner. Robesonians have also proved helpful to the county in Washington, D.C. They include people like Frank Ertle Carlyle, Gilbert Brown Patterson, Mike McIntyre, and Angus Dhu McLean, who served as assistant attorney general.

Shown is the official seal of
Robeson County.

The second Robeson County Courthouse was built in 1848 to replace the original courthouse, which had become expensive to maintain and repair. In 1851 *The Fayetteville Observer* reported "the new courthouse is finished and is a handsome building and probably larger that any other in the circuit, but is not as convenient as some we have seen . . . we understand that it cost $7,500". (Courtesy Historical Robeson, Inc.)

Robeson County saw the need for a new courthouse and constructed this one in 1909. This side view from the 1950s shows not only the wonderful courthouse that served the county until 1969 but also a downtown garage. This seat of county government continues to serve the people of the State of Robeson as it has since Gen. John Willis gave the land in 1787. (Courtesy Carolina Collection, UNC-Chapel Hill.)

Built originally to house the fire department, this building once housed the Robeson County public library. Fireman Rudolph Lewis spoke fondly of his service to the department and remembers that the Carolina Theatre use to provide two movie tickets a week to the firemen. (Courtesy Historical Robeson, Inc.)

The Robeson County Health Department, organized in 1912, was the first county health department in the United States. When Dr. B.W. Page was hired on February 19, 1912, he started addressing the country's health problems, including typhoid fever, hookworm disease, unsanitary conditions, smallpox, and high infant death. The current building was named for Dr. Eugene Ramsey Hardin, the third county health director. (Courtesy Historical Robeson, Inc.)

Four of the county's five commissioners gathered on the steps of the courthouse to have their photograph taken for a special issue of *The Robesonian* that was published May 6, 1915. From left to right are chairman A.J. Floyd, J.F. McKay, J.W. Ward, and Rory McNair. C.B. Townsend was sick and unable to be there that day. (Courtesy Historical Robeson, Inc.)

James A. Kitchen, son of John Kitchen and Mary Ann McLean, was born September 28, 1861 and on April 12, 1894 married Flora Cattie Monroe. Kitchen served as deputy sheriff of Robeson County and was killed in the line of duty on July 3, 1920 by John Henry Bethea. Bethea and his brother were driving a car filled with 5 gallons of whiskey and 100 pounds of sugar. John Henry Bethea surrendered to South Carolina officials on July 24, 1920. (Courtesy of Victoria Smith.)

Pictured in front of the Robeson County Jail, from left to right, are Anna Ivey Prevatte; her husband Archibald Prevatte; Alfred Rowland Pittman; and Iola Ivey Pittman, wife of Alfred Rowland Pittman and sister of Anna Ivey Prevatte. Archibald Prevatte served as jailer for the county during Prohibition. (Courtesy of David Mann.)

In this 1874 report of the Robeson County Grand Jury, it was reported that they had visited and inspected the county jail and found it well kept but insecure. (Courtesy Hubbard-Tyner Collection.)

Angus Wilton McLean was born in Robeson County on April 20, 1870 to Archibald and Carolina Amanda Purcell McLean. He received his law degree from the University of North Carolina in 1892 and in 1917 was elected president of the state bar. He married Margaret Jones French on April 14, 1904; she stood beside her husband while he served as assistant Secretary of the Treasury in Washington and when he was elected as governor of North Carolina in 1925. McLean organized many of the county's business such as the National Bank of Lumberton in 1897, which later became Southern National Bank; the Lumberton and Dresden Cotton Mills; and the Virginia & Carolina Southern Railroad. Gov. Angus Wilton McLean was claimed by death on June 20 1935. (Courtesy North Carolina State Archives.)

This photograph of Hector MacLean, son of Gov. Angus Wilton McLean, and the proceeding photograph were taken on February 18, 1928. The occasion was the installation of the first telephones in the Governor's Mansion. Hector is shown here making a call to his father's office in the Capital Building. Hector MacLean was the youngest of the three McLean children. His sister referred to him in later years as "a breath of fresh air into the family." His mother was known for lavish entertaining, and both parents loved animals. Mrs. McLean always had pet dogs and Governor McLean was an expert horseman. The children even kept their pony in the basement of the Governor's Mansion. The pony and the mansion grounds were cared for by a group of prisoners known as "trustees." Hector MacLean traveled almost everywhere with his father and was even by his side at the unveiling of the North Carolina Monument at Gettysburg. MacLean graduated from the School of Law at the University of North Carolina at Chapel Hill and served four years in the army during World War II. After the war he took the reins of his father's bank and by the time of his retirement the bank had grown to over 100 branches. He has continued his father's example of service to the community by being active in the preservation of county and state history. (Courtesy North Carolina State Archives.)

Angus L. Shaw was a leading political figure in Robeson County. He served as the first mayor of Lumber Bridge in 1891, was county commissioner from 1898 until 1905, and served as chairman from 1900 until 1902. Shaw was later elected to represent Robeson County as a state senator. He was brother of Laughlin Shaw of St. Pauls. (Courtesy Historical Robeson, Inc.)

Hamilton McMillan was born August 29, 1837 and in 1873 married Elizabeth Gillespie Robeson, great-granddaughter of Col. Thomas Robeson. Hamilton served Robeson County in the state legislature 1885–1887, during which time he became interested in the Indians of Robeson County. He was convinced that they were the descendants of the "Lost Colony" and in 1888 published a monograph, *Sir Walter Raleigh's Lost Colony*. He introduced a bill on March 7, 1887 to create a school for the Indians. This lead to what is now the University of North Carolina at Pembroke. (Courtesy UNCP University Relations.)

Six

MILITARY

The men and women of Robeson County have been active in all of the nation's wars. Robesonians marched off during the Revolution to free us from British rule and then during the Civil War for state's rights. Robeson County and the nation were drawn into World Wars I and II, with many brave soldiers paying the high price of freedom with their life. The Korean Conflict and Vietnam once again drew on the brave of Robeson to fight. One unique war was Robeson's internal war known as "The Lowery War," which lasted 10 years and saw bloodshed from the whites and Native Americans.

The Laurinburg-Maxton Air Base was home to the largest training facility in the country for glider pilots. Their unit patch features a mule pulling two gliders. (Courtesy of Maxton Historical Society.)

On September 1, 1781 British Colonel Fanning's men defeated the Whig forces at McPhaul's Mill. During this time William Lowrie, grandfather of Henry Berry Lowery, was piloting Colonel Wade's men across Drowning Creek when he was attacked by Tory James McPherson. He received a severe sword cut to his left hand and was said to have been granted a federal pension. (Courtesy Hubbard-Tyner Collection.)

On October 15, 1871, Patriot forces caught up with the Tory forces near Raft Swamp. The Tories, seeing that they were about to be defeated, tried to cross Raft Swamp; however, it was not to be and fighting continued until dark. The Tories had 16 men killed and 50 wounded; the Patriots suffered 2 broken swords. (Courtesy Hubbard-Tyner Collection.)

Dr. James Dallas Croom, son of John Bunyan and Mary Jane McDuffie, was born on February 12, 1822. His first medical experience came at the age of 16 when he volunteered for the Civil War. He served as a doctor in Maxton for years, even starting a local hospital. He married Anna Mortimer Blake, and they were parents of four sons and a daughter. He named one of his sons after his commanding officer, Maj. Robert DeVane. His sons continued in the medical field; Robert DeVane Croom was a pharmacist, James Dallas Croom Jr. was a dentist, and Arthur Bascom Croom was a medical doctor. Grandsons Robert DeVane Croom Jr. and Arthur Bascom Croom Jr. also became medical doctors. (Courtesy Maxton Historical Society.)

I. _Margaret Hampfield_ of _Robeson_ County, State of North-Carolina, do solemnly swear or affirm in presence of Almighty God, that I will henceforth faithfully support, protect and defend the Constitution of the United States and the Union of the States thereunder; and that I will, in like manner, abide by and faithfully support all laws and proclamations which have been made during the existing rebellion with reference to the emancipation of slaves. So help me God.

Margaret Hampfield

Sworn and subscribed to this the ___11___ day of ___September___, A. D., 1865, before

A. McGirt, J. P.

It is hereby certified that the above is a true copy of the original oath taken and subscribed by _Margaret Hampfield_

A. McGirt, J. P.

W. D. Caldwell, J. P.

After the Civil War, Southerners were required to sign Oaths of Allegiance. Margaret Campbell appeared before Justices of the Peace A. McGirt and W.D. Caldwell on September 21, 1865 to sign her oath. It stated that she would faithfully support, protect, and defend the Constitution of the United States and the Union of States. It also stated that she must support all laws and proclamations, which had been made during the rebellion, with reference to the emancipation of slaves. (Courtesy Mary McLean Poole Collection, Maxton Historical Society.)

Robeson County's Confederate veterans gathered in 1916 on the steps of the courthouse just a few feet away from the Confederate Memorial that was dedicated in 1907. This photograph was published in the February 24, 1953 issue of *The Robesonian* with no identifications. In the days following, the paper received letters from citizens offering names of some of the veterans. In the front row from left to right are ? Wilkins, Joseph Ratley, S.S. (Strong) Wishart, Isham Lamb, Rev. Furney Prevatte, Calvin Smith, unidentified, H.G. Byrd or Alfred Prevatte, and two unidentified man. In the second row are unidentified, William Haywood Graham, Michael Bullock, A.B. Small, five unidentified men, Steven Lawson, and Ben Parnell. In the third row are unidentified, William Townsend, an unidentified woman, Rev. F.A. Prevatte, William P. Norton, three unidentified people, W.H. Barnes, J.T. Prevatte or Henry Spivey, and Duckery Allen. (Courtesy Historical Robeson, Inc.)

The monument to honor the Confederate soldiers of Robeson County was unveiled in front of the Robeson County Courthouse on Confederate Memorial Day, May 10, 1907. (Courtesy of Historic Robeson, Inc.)

Samuel Goodwin Hubbard (June 2, 1838–October 12, 1906), son of Peter S. Hubbard and Matilda Jane Goodwin, was born in Marlboro County, South Carolina. While serving the South in the Civil War, he lost a leg. He married first Flora Louise Burn; they were the parents of ten children. After the birth of their last child, Flora knew she was dying. At her request made on her deathbed, Samuel married Miss Mary Belle Patterson. (Courtesy of Joanne B. Harley.)

This drawing was done for Sidney Hubbard in 1916 while serving in Co. F, Second North Carolina in America's Mexican boarder conflict. It shows a stylized Mexican soldier with all his equipment. (Courtesy Hubbard-Tyner Collection.)

John Gilchrist Hughes, son of Dr. Daniel Hughes and Carrie McKinnon, was active in lumber, farming, and mercantile businesses. He served 12 years as chairman of the Robeson County Board of Commissioners. This father of five entered the army during World War I; during the war his sixth child, Robert Archibald Hughes, was born. The name John Gilchrist Hughes has continued in the family and John Gilchrist Hughes V just celebrated his 5th birthday. (Courtesy Mary Shaw Hughes.)

Ella Currie McKay Pellegrini, R.N. (1888–1974) was the daughter of James Franklin McKay and Ann Flora McPherson McKay of Philadelphus, Robeson County and the wife of Francis X. Pellegrini of Philadelphia, Pennsylvania. She graduated from Flora MacDonald College before attending nursing school in Salisbury, North Carolina. She worked as a Red Cross nurse at the Confederate Soldier's Home in Raleigh from 1916 to 1918 and during World War I. (Courtesy McKay Family Photograph Collection, in the possession of S.C. Edgerton.)

William Peter McKay (1893–1960), known to all as "Dr. Pete," was the son of James Franklin McKay and Ann Flora McPherson McKay of Philadelphus, Robeson County. He married Gladys Toon of Red Springs. McKay served as a physician in France during World War I and was one of the founders of Highsmith's Hospital in Fayetteville. (Courtesy McKay Family Photograph Collection, in the possession of S.C. Edgerton.)

Walter Alexander Fowler (June 12, 1892–September 7, 1971), son of Sandy Alexander Fowler and Katherine McDuffie, married Frances M. Ray. They and their five children made their home on a Saddletree farm. Fowler fought bravely for his country during World War I; his son, Henry Joseph Fowler, fought in World War II and earned a Purple Heart.

Pvt. Watus Prevatte was born in 1898 and lost his life while fighting for the United States in France during World War I on October 10, 1918. His body was brought back and reinterred at Meadowbrook Cemetery in Lumberton, c. 1921. (Courtesy North Carolina State Archives.)

John Hector Shaw Sr. was the son of John Calvin Shaw and Laura Kate Bethune. He served his country during World War I. (Courtesy Mary Shaw Hughes.)

The mourners of Pvt. Watus Prevatte are shown displaying the flag that was draped over his casket. The Prevatte family in Robeson County stretches back to brothers Thomas and Peter Prevatte. They were the great-grandsons of Pierre Prevol, who was born in 1673 in Guines Pas-De-Calais, France and came to the New World in 1700. He and the other Huguenots settled in Manakintown, Virginia. (Courtesy North Carolina State Archives.)

Simeon Oxendine, a Pembroke native, enlisted in the Air Force in September 1939, two years before the United States was drawn into the war. Oxendine served aboard a B-17 "Flying Fortress" as a member of "Hell's Angels," which was the first group to fly 100 missions. He was awarded the Distinguished Flying Cross and received a Presidential Citation for destroying a German ball-bearing plant at Swinesworth, Germany. (Courtesy UNCP University Relations.)

Robert Rudolph Lewis was born in Lumberton on September 2, 1906 to Warren and Lillie Spivey Lewis, and married Esther Hazel Stevens in Dillon, South Carolina on May 28, 1928. After their marriage they made their home in Lumberton where they owned a grocery store/restaurant beside the Carolina Theater. His World War II service was as a guard at the Prisoner of War Camp in South Carolina. (Courtesy Hubbard-Tyner Collection.)

Clyde Tyner was born on December 17, 1924 in Dillon, South Carolina to Archibald Blue Tyner and Claudia Snipes. He served his country in Germany during World War II, for which he received a Purple Heart, and he reenlisted during the Korean Conflict. He married Harriett Lewis and had two daughters and two sons. This photograph was taken during World War II and sent home to his mother. (Courtesy Hubbard-Tyner Collection.)

James H. Oxendine, a 1938 graduate of the Indian Normal School of Robeson County, served as a communications sergeant for Company B of the United States 630th Tank Destroyer Battalion. He was awarded the European Campaign Medal with five bronze stars, the American Theater Campaign Medal, the American Defense Medal, the Victory Medal, the Good Conduct Medal, and a France decoration. (Courtesy UNCP University Relations.)

Ewing Cox of Red Springs fought bravely for his country during World War II and was awarded a Purple Heart. (Courtesy Red Springs Historical Museum.)

Walter Cox, son of Ewing Cox, went to Vietnam to fight on behalf of his country. While stationed there, he was wounded three times and received three Purple Hearts. On one occasion his dog tags were hit by a bullet, thus stopping what could have been a more serious injury. (Courtesy Red Springs Historical Museum.)

Maj. Alexander L. Lewis, a Lumberton native, was serving as post chaplain of the United States Army Garrison Fort Hamilton in August 1958 when he was alerted that he would be leaving for Korea. He was the only African American holding this type of position in the army. Lewis had served in combat in Europe and the Pacific, where he was awarded a bronze and silver star. (Courtesy Historic Robeson, Inc.)

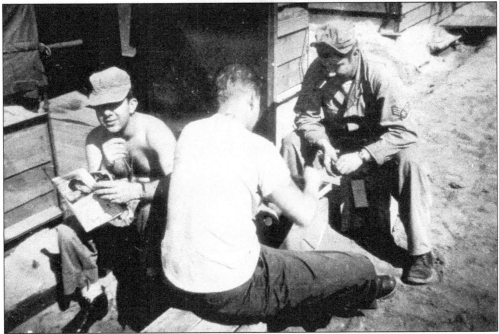

Billy Franklin Sibbette (in uniform), a St. Pauls native and son of Dennis and Pearl Beard Sibbette, takes time off during the Korea Conflict to play checkers with C.G. Fell of Flat Rock, Michigan at the Kimpo Air Force Base. Harold Anderson of Rocky Mount, North Carolina sits nearby, reading. (Courtesy Hubbard-Tyner Collection.)

Red Springs native Rebecca Black served her country during the Korean War. (Courtesy Red Springs Historical Museum.)

Jimmy Locklear was born November 20, 1949 and lived in Maxton before joining the army and achieving the rank of SP4 (E4). He fought bravely for his country before paying the price of freedom with his life on September 4, 1968 at the age of 18 in the Hug Nghia Province of South Vietnam. His name is carved into the Vietnam Memorial Wall on Panel 45W, Row 38. (Courtesy Jimmy Locklear.)

The Lumberton Battery B of the National Guard is shown firing a 10-inch rifle in August 1925 at Fort Monroe, Virginia. (Courtesy Historic Robeson, Inc.)

The former Parkton National Guard building was completed in 1940 and was home for years to the Scottish Tigers. This brave regiment was chartered as the Lumber Bridge Independent Light Infantry, Company L during the Mexican War on October 12, 1847 with Capt. Arch Malloy as their first commander. They received their name during the Civil War when Gen. Robert E. Lee commented to their commander A.A. McKeithan, "Your regiment fights like tigers and holds their ground like they have tar on their heels." McKeithan replied, "That's right we are the 'Scottish Tigers,'" and the name has held. (Courtesy Historical Robeson, Inc.)

The Laurinburg-Maxton Air Base, the largest Glider Training facility in the country, was built partly on property purchased and leased to the government by Maxton, Laurinburg, and Robeson and Scotland Counties. Base Photographer Sgt. Charles E. Darneal took all of the photographs on these two pages. He climbed in the Flying Fortress to take an aerial photograph of two gliders being towed by a bomber. What he thought would be a quick spin found him a 110 miles away in Columbia. He was A.W.O.L. but since the photograph was so good, all was forgiven. (Sgt. Charles E. Darneal Collection, Maxton Historical Society.)

The air base was constructed at a cost of $10 million dollars and netted 20 miles of paved roads within the compound. The sudden influx of 6,000–8,000 men and their families into the area caused problems unlike any the surrounding area had ever experienced. Almost every home in Maxton made rooms available to rent. Here we see many of those men practicing their jumping skills. (Sgt. Charles E. Darneal Collection, Maxton Historical Society.)

Many high-ranking officials visited the base during its years of operation. After World War II, the base was considered surplus property and was turned over to Maxton and Laurinburg. In the autumn of 1947 a corporation called Airports Operations, Inc., owned by the Presbyterian Junior College, operated the airport. They used it for an aviation educational program. In 1948, Maxton transferred the air base hospital property to the Scotland County Memorial Hospital. Also in 1948, Maxton and Laurinburg entered into an agreement to form the Laurinburg-Maxton Airport Commission to administer the airport property. (Sgt. Charles E. Darneal Collection, Maxton Historical Society.)

The Associated Press picked up this photograph showing Santa driving a jeep off of a glider at the Laurinburg-Maxton Air Base during the Christmas 1944 season. Sergeant Darneal was recognized for taking such a wonderful photograph. He had worked eight years at Louisville's *Courier-Journal* before the onset of World War II. (Sgt. Charles E. Darneal Collection, Maxton Historical Society.)

Henry Berry Lowery was the leader of the Lowery Gang. He was son of Allen Lowery and great-grandson of James Lowrie, who had operated a tavern during the Revolutionary War. Henry Berry Lowery married Rhoda Strong, who was known for her beauty. Lowery and his gang spent a ten-year period stealing from Robeson County citizens. He was arrested for the murder of postmaster James P. Barnes but escaped from the Whiteville jail in which he was being held. He disappeared and many opinions have developed over the years to explain his absence. Some say he was accidentally killed and buried by his gang members, while others say he escaped to the North. (Courtesy Historic Robeson, Inc.)

Francis Marion Wishart was born in Robeson County and fought to defend his homeland during the Civil War. In January 1866 he married Lydia Pitman, with whom he had been in love for several years. He had to steal her from under the watchful eye of Mrs. Pitman, who could not bring herself to approve of a son-in-law as audacious as Wishart, but love finds a way and Frank became a favorite in the Pitman home. He opened a store in the newly formed village of Shoe Heel but finding no place to live, rented a house near Floral College. On August 18, 1870 he was placed in charge of the Robeson County Militia by Governor Holden to deal with the problem of Henry Berry Lowery and his band of outlaws. On July 10, 1871 Wishart and his militia captured the wives of the Lowery band and placed them in the Robeson County jail. On August 18, 1871 Governor Caldwell promoted Wishart to the rank of colonel. On May 2, 1872 death came to Col. Francis Marion Wishart. He had received word to come to Scuffletown and meet with the Lowery Outlaws, but he was ambushed near Lebanon Presbyterian Church and killed. Wishart's son, William Clifford Wishart, became vice president of the New York Central Railroad. After Wishart's death, Lydia married W.B. Harker, editor of *The Scottish Chief*. (Courtesy Wishart Family Papers, Southern Historical Collection, UNC-Chapel Hill.)

Three members of the Robeson County Militia take time out from stalking the Lowery Gang to pose for a photograph. (Courtesy Wishart Family Papers, Southern Historical Collection, UNC-Chapel Hill.)

THOMAS LOWERY.

Thomas Lowery was a brother of Henry Berry Lowery. On July 18, 1872 he visited the home of Furney Prevatt. When the militia learned of this, they waited nearby for him. The next morning, Thomas Lowery was killed on his way to Union Chapel by James McKay. His body was taken to Lumberton in order for the group to claim the $6,000 reward. Lowery was 37 at the time of his death. (Courtesy *Harper's Weekly*.)

John S. McNeill, Angus Archie McNeill, William McNeill, John K. McNeill, Alexander McNeill, Daniel McNeill, Hector McNeill, David McNeill, Archie D. McCallum, W. Frierson Buie, Frank McKay, George W. McKay, and Archibald Brown captured Henderson Oxendine, a member of the Lowery Gang, on February 26, 1871. They took him to Lumberton where on April 15, 1871 he was found guilty of crimes ranging from robbery to murder. He was sentenced to hang and before his death gave a full confession. (Courtesy *Harper's Weekly*.)

HENDERSON OXENDINE.

This tintype shows James Franklin "Frank" McKay (1849–1941), son of Duncan McKay and Harriett McNeill McKay; Archie (Archibald Davis) McCallum (1849–1913), son of James McCallum and Catherine Anne Smith McCallum and husband of Mary Attelia Blue; and William McCallum (1844–1923), son of James McCallum and Catherine Anne Smith McCallum. They were in the posse that pursued the Henry Berry Lowery Gang, and this photograph was taken around that time period, 1870–1872. (Courtesy McKay Family Photograph Collection in the possession of S.C. Edgerton.)

CALVIN OXENDINE.

Calvin Oxendine was part of Henry Berry Lowery's band of outlaw/hero Lumbee Indians. The gang had a long-running feud with the Confederate Home Guard in Robeson County, North Carolina. (Courtesy *Harper's Weekly*.)

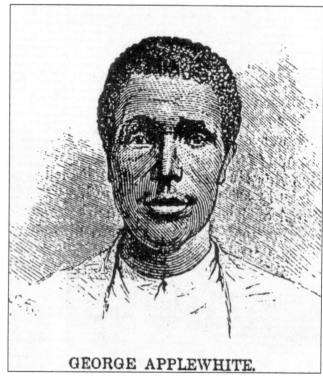

GEORGE APPLEWHITE.

George Applewhite, an African American, was a member of the Lowery Gang. This gang has often been compared to Robin Hood. (Courtesy *Harper's Weekly*.)

This woodcut showing the community of Moss Neck, along with the ones on the three preceding pages, appeared in an article about the Lowery Gang in the March 30, 1872 issue of *Harper's Weekly*. (Courtesy *Harper's Weekly*.)

A group of Robeson County men calling themselves the Red Shirt Brigade formed to respond to the appointment of a large number of African Americans to county government offices. Graham McCallum and George A. McKay are shown in their Red Shirts Uniforms. The inscription on the back of the photograph reads "Remember the Red Shirts of 98 who held Robeson & saved the State. What fools we mortals were in the year 98 to hold the county of Robeson and save the Old North State." (Courtesy McKay Family Photograph Collection in the possession of S.C. Edgerton.)

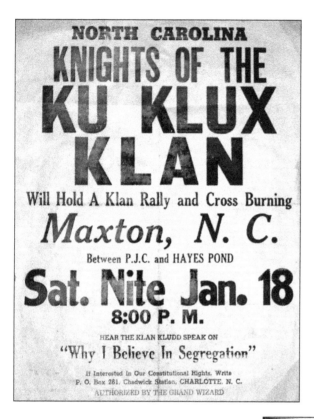

For weeks leading up to January 18, 1958, members of the Knights of the Ku Klux Klan had been sending flyers like this to advertise a rally to be held in Maxton. Maxton chief of police Bob Fisher sent letters to surrounding law enforcement agencies, including the state police and Federal Bureau of Investigation, asking for their help to prevent the expected racial violence. The Native American men of the area made up their minds to end the Klan's activities in this area. (Courtesy Native American Resource Center, UNCP.)

The Klansmen were confronted by the Native Americans, angry words were exchanged, and shots were fired into the air. The Klan disbursed, leaving behind their flag and cross. As word of the fight against the Klan spread across the country, *Life* magazine carried two separate articles on the subject. Letters poured into the area from all over the country, most of them in support of the Native Americans. The Klan did not really die that night, but it did apparently learn to stay out of Indian Country. (Courtesy Native American Resource Center, UNCP.)

Seven

ROBESON COUNTY CITIZENS

The story of Robeson County is a rich tapestry woven of the threads of individual life stories of each of its citizens. From farmers to textile workers, teachers to doctors, each Robesonian has contributed to the history and development of the county.

On December 1, 1952 a pageant was held at the Lumberton High School to celebrate the centennial of the founding of Lumberton. Representing the Scottish settlers of the county were John Luther McLean, his wife Isabel McLean, and their son, Marshall McLean. W.F. Floyd was chosen to represent the Huguenot settlers. (Courtesy Historical Robeson, Inc.)

99

Anderson N. Locklear, the son of John Archie and Margaret Locklear, was born August 14, 1870. He entered the Croatan Normal School when it was founded in 1887 and was one of its first graduates. He spent 42 years teaching and served on the Board of Trustees of Pembroke State University for 22 years, until his death in 1934. They honored his memory with the naming of Locklear Hall. (Courtesy UNCP University Relations.)

All of the Davis Brothers were born in Robeson County. From left to right are (first row) John and Fredrick; (second row) Lock and William. William first married Temperance Council, and they made their home of St. Pauls at the site of the original St. Pauls Presbyterian Church. (Courtesy Red Springs Historical Museum.)

Prof. John Truman Peterson became principal of the Red Springs black school in 1933; this was the year the first high school class graduated. His entire mission was to provide a quality education for Red Springs African-American children. On July 1, 1958 the new high school was named in his honor. With the 1969 integration of the school system the Peterson High School became the Peterson Elementary School. The building was destroyed March 28, 1984 when a tornado ripped through the town. The new Peterson Elementary School was opened for students on September 2, 1986. (Courtesy Red Springs Historical Museum.)

James McNatt was born on December 1, 1821 and on December 10, 1846 married Janet McGeachy. He was a large landowner in the northern part of the county, and McNatt's Station on the Cape Fear and Yadkin Valley Railroad was named in his honor. His turpentine still was burned by Sherman's troops as they marched through the area. (Courtesy John and Dot Ray.)

Nancy Dallas McPherson (1797–1875) was the daughter of Peter Dallas and the wife of Alexander McPherson. Nancy and Alexander were parents of Daniel McPherson; Hugh McPherson, CSA; Sarah McPherson Leach; Gilbert Gilchrist McPherson, CSA (shown on page 18 with his large family); John Archibald McPherson, CSA; Catherine McPherson Buie; Colin Alexander McPherson, CSA; Ann Jane McPherson Buie; Neil Archibald McPherson; and Mary Eliza McPherson Brown. (Courtesy McKay Family Photograph Collection in the possession of S.C. Edgerton.)

Alexander McPherson (1798–1879) was the youngest child of Daniel McPherson and Marron (Sarah) McNeill McPherson of Robeson County and the grandson of John McPherson of the Argyll Colony. He was a brother of Mary McPherson Gilchrist, Nancy McPherson Gilchrist, Catherine McPherson Brown, Flora McPherson Buie, Archibald McPherson, Neill McPherson, Hugh McPherson, and Colin McPherson. Both Alexander and his wife, Nancy, are buried at Philadelphus Church cemetery. (Courtesy McKay Family Photograph Collection in the possession of S.C. Edgerton.)

Dr. Joy Johnson graduated from the Laurinburg Institute and then attended Shaw University. He was called to the First Baptist Church in Fairmont in September 1951. He was active in his community, serving as state secretary of the NAACP, president of the Robeson County Black Caucus, and founder of the African American Cultural Center in Lumberton. He was elected the first black mayor of Fairmont. (Courtesy African American Cultural Center.)

This Lumbee couple, Archibald Oxendine and wife Margaret Ann Lowery, sat for a photograph c. 1875. (Courtesy UNCP University Relations.)

Pembroke native Bill Lowery is shown with Dr. C.C. Crittenden viewing an antique gun at North Carolina Hall of History in 1959; Lowery was 98 at the time. (Courtesy North Carolina State Archives.)

Lewis Edward Tyner and his wife Martha Barnes were supporters of Campbell College, where he spent several years on the board of trustees. After their deaths their children Walter Ray Tyner, Belle Tyner Johnson, Bunyan Yates Tyner, Addie Tyner Baucon, Edna Tyner Langston, Dr. Carl Vann Tyner, and Cora Leigh Tyner Pittman established an endowed chair for the religion department in their parents' name. (Courtesy Historical Robeson, Inc.)

104

Margaret Dalrymple McNair (1787–1882) was the daughter of patriot Col. Archibald Dalrymple and wife of Malcolm McNair. She was the mother of Catherine Gaster McNair McKinnon, Mary Ann McNair McIver, Dr. Archibald Dalrymple McNair, and Rev. John Calvin McNair. Reverend McNair left a legacy in his will to establish a series of lectures on science and theology at the University of North Carolina, where he graduated in 1849. (Courtesy North Carolina State Archives.)

Rev. Charles G. Vardell, longtime head of Flora MacDonald College, spends part of the afternoon talking with Tom Brown on his front porch. (Courtesy Red Springs Historical Museum.)

Carrie B. Miller was born in Durham and was trained as a teacher. She moved to Maxton where she married Richard McEachern on November 14, 1895. They had one daughter, Marie, born on October 12, 1903. Mrs. McEachern taught at Maxton Schools for several years. (Courtesy Peggy Tyner Townsend.)

Benjamin Tyner Jr. was born in 1790 in Johnston County and died in 1883 in Robeson County. His great-great-grandfather Nicholas Tyner died in 1708 in Isle of Wight County, Virginia. Benjamin was father of four sons— Nicholas, James, William, and Benjamin—and two daughters—Elizabeth and Margaret. His son Benjamin died in Richmond, Virginia during the Civil War. This photograph was taken in Richmond when he went to try and recover the son's body. (Courtesy Peggy Tyner Townsend.)

THE NORTH CAROLINA SOCIETY

OF THE

COLONIAL DAMES OF AMERICA

ANNOUNCE THE UNVEILING BY

THE RICHMOND-ROBESON COUNTY COMMITTEE

OF A MARKER TO

JAMES ROBERT ADAIR, M. D.

ON THURSDAY, THE SECOND OF AUGUST

AT ELEVEN O'CLOCK

ROWLAND, NORTH CAROLINA

In August of 1934 the Robeson-Richmond Committee of the North Carolina Society Colonial Dames of America unveiled a historical marker in honor of James Robert Adair, a pioneer physician, patriot, and author of *History of American Indians*, published in London in 1775. Mrs. N.A. McLean of Lumberton presided over the event with Miss Mary Harllee of New Orleans and Miss Jane Alford of Rowland having the honor of unveiling their ancestor's marker. (Courtesy Historic Robeson, Inc.)

Prior to the unveiling of this marker, Dr. Adair's history and achievements were extolled at a program held at Ashpole Church. Speakers included Dr. A.R. Newsome, secretary of the state historical commission; Fort Bragg Brig. Gen. Manus McClosky; Dr. McCain, head of state tubercular sanatorium and president-elect of state medical society; Col. William Curry Harllee, author of *Kinfolks*; and Mr. C.J. McCallum, elder of Ashpole Church. (Courtesy Hubbard-Tyner Collection.)

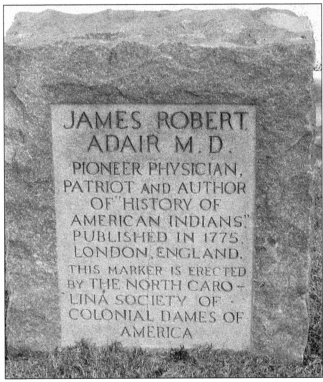

All schools are constantly looking for queens to represent them. Miss Sybil Lowery was crowned Miss Prospect High for 1974–1975. (Courtesy Historic Robeson.)

Lorna McNeill (below, left) was crowned Miss North Carolina 2000. She was the first Native American and native Robesonian to win the title. Rebecca Revels (below, right) won Miss North Carolina 2002. McNeill serves as the alumni director of her alma mater, the University of North Carolina at Pembroke, while Revels is an English teacher at her former high school in St. Pauls. (Courtesy UNCP University Relations.)

Morris Marley, a leading merchant of Lumber Bridge, married Margaret Smith, daughter of Col. Peter P. Smith. He built a large Victorian house on the road leading from Parkton to Red Springs; his 1908 Buick was one of the first cars in Lumber Bridge. (Courtesy Bardell Collection, Maxton Historical Society.)

In 1917 Mr. and Mrs. E.L. Odum donated 58 acres of land in Pembroke for use as a Indian orphanage. It was 31 years later that four young Indian girls became the first residents of the Odum Children's Home. In 1958 the home became part of the Baptist Children's Homes of North Carolina. (Courtesy UNCP University Relations.)

Rosezile "Zilie" Locklear Jones (December 22, 1878–February 25, 1958) was the daughter of Hitchner Locklear (c. 1830–December 22, 1905) and Sylvania Locklear (c. 1834–May 6, 1906). Zilie married William Jones (March 15, 1872–November 23, 1955), son of Polly Ann Jones, and they lived in the St. Annah Church community north of Pembroke. (Courtesy Lawrence Locklear.)

John Daniel McRainey, son of John McRainey and Flora McMillian, was born on his family's farm several miles north of St. Pauls. He married Carolina Victoria McNeill and at his father's death purchased the farm from his siblings. He invested in the Parkton Telephone Company and when it fell into financial trouble in 1912 he kept the bills paid and the company running. After his death it was taken over by his son, John Hector McRainey. It was sold in the late 1950s to Carolina Telephone. (Courtesy Faye McRainey Reaves.)

J.W. Carter was a leading merchant in both Maxton and Fairmont. He served as mayor of Maxton and chairman of the Robeson County Commissioners. He married Lena Alford, daughter of Henry Clay Alford and Clarkie Jane McKay. Carter was also a large financial supporter of the St. Pauls Methodist Church and Carolina College, both in Maxton. (Courtesy Carter Collection, Maxton Historical Society.)

On March 11, 1775, "Sailor" Hector McNeill received a large land grant for what is now Red Springs. His grandson "Red" Hector McNeill became the first mayor of Red Springs when it was incorporated in 1887. (Courtesy Red Springs Historical Museum.)

Staff Sgt. Norman Hubert Bunnell, son of Norman and Macy Davis Bunnell, is shown on maneuvers at Fort Jackson, South Carolina. While stationed in Europe, Bunnell was awarded a Bronze Star on March 27, 1945 for leading an attack of the enemy. The enemy counter attacked and Bunnell was forced to call for support. He rallied his squad, and they fought 45 minutes until backup arrived. (Courtesy John and Dot Ray.)

Bruce Stuart Roberts and Nancy Roberts are caught on the other side of the camera for once. He is known for the wonderful photographs he has taken all over the South, while she is known for the more than 20 books she has authored on Southern ghosts and folklore. For a time they published the *Scottish Chief* in Maxton. She has dedicated her life to gathering the South's legends, and he served as director of photography at *Southern Living* from 1963 until 1978. (Courtesy Maxton Historical Society.)

Dr. Daniel Hughes (1836–1918), the son of Effie Gilchrist and John Hughes, married Carrie McKinnon in 1869. He followed in his mother's double-first cousin Dr. Daniel Gilchrist's footsteps and entered the field of dentistry. Before his death in 1875, Dr. Gilchrist sent most of his dental instruments to Dr. Hughes. The Hughes were parents of Mary Bethune Hughes Cobb, John Gilchrist Hughes, Gilbert Cobb Hughes, Luther Evander Hughes, and Emma Hurst Hughes. (Courtesy Mary Neill Shaw Hughes.)

Four female friends take time from studying to be photographed. From left to right are Mary Janet McNeil, Margaret Gillis, Beatrice McEachern, and Miss Finley. (Courtesy John and Dot Ray.)

John Archibald Gillis, son of David Chase Gillis and Christian Black, was born on July 27, 1839 and died August 26, 1903. He married Catherine Ann McNatt, daughter of James McNatt and Janet McGeachy. He is shown here with St. Pauls businessman Locke Shaw. (Courtesy John and Dot Ray.)

James C. Dobbin McNatt, who built and operated McNatt's Hotel in Parkton for years, is shown with his sisters, Cornelia McNatt Livingston (left) and Catherine Ann McNatt Gillis (right). They were the children of James McNatt (1821–1887) and Janet McGeachy McNatt (1819–1862). (Courtesy John and Dot Ray.)

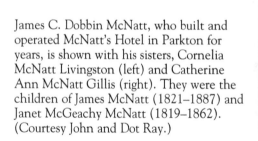

Eight

SOCIAL AND COMMUNITY EVENTS

Social and Community events have been held along the Lumber River since before the county was formed from Bladen. Robesonians are drawn to water, be it the river or a fishing pond. A rich source of hunting was quickly found in the woods and swamps of the county. Many important celebrations have been held in the county, from the centennials of Lumberton and Maxton to the 50th anniversary of Rowland. And who can forget the 1987 bicentennial celebration of the county itself?

The Lumbee Homecoming is held annually in late June and early July of each year. One of the highlights is the Pow Wow. (Courtesy of UNCP University Relations.)

This photograph was originally owned by Miss Elizabeth Wishart, daughter of W.S. Wishart, and shows what could have been the *Kitty B*, which was known to travel the waters of the Lumber River. This 60-foot, flat-bottom square-ender more than likely was used to handle logs down the river during the week and used for pleasure-seekers on the weekends. (Courtesy Historic Robeson, Inc.)

This celebration, where Sixth Street in Lumberton meets the banks of the Lumber River, occurred *c.* 1917 and was probably a May Day celebration, due to the fact that the girls are going around and around a May Pole. (Courtesy Historic Robeson, Inc.)

Lumberton photographer Lillian Ferguson must have viewed this as a scene that could not be passed when she captured these two young boys fishing alongside the famous lumber bridge, from which the town of Lumber Bridge takes its name. (Courtesy Historic Robeson, Inc.)

An unidentified gentleman looks content to row these lovely ladies around the Moss Neck Pond. While Stella McNeill Chandler fishes, Quissie Ratley McNeill serves as a lookout with her rifle to take care of any snakes that might happen along. Snakes have always been a problem in Robeson County. Educator Charles Hunter mentions in his memoirs that he saw more snakes in his three-year stay in Robeson than he had ever seen. (Courtesy Peggy Tyner Townsend.)

When Robesonians leave the county on vacation, they have always seemed to flock to water. Our close proximity to the beaches makes it an easy day trip. John Hector McRainey of St. Pauls is seen here with his young son, John Neill McRainey. The McRainey family settled north of St. Pauls in the community of Athens and farmed a large estate for years. They also operated the Parkton Telephone Company. (Courtesy Faye McRainey Reaves.)

Esther Stephens, a native of Loris, South Carolina, moved to St. Pauls with her parents, where she finished school. In 1928 she married Lumberton native Rudolph Lewis. For several years they operated a cafe and grocery store beside the Carolina Civic Center. This photograph was taken along the boardwalk of Myrtle Beach in the 1930s. (Courtesy Hubbard-Tyner Collection.)

Hunting was always necessary to provide food for the family table, but in the late 1800s the sport of hunting was born in the South and lasts until today. Robert Lide Burn Jr. sent this photograph to his double-first cousin, Flora Burn Hubbard, at Purvis. He was the son of Robert Lide Burn Sr. and Sarah Roberts Burn. She is the daughter of Rev. John Wilson Burn and Susan Roberts Burn. (Courtesy Hubbard-Tyner Collection.)

Roscoe B. Tolar grew up in the Rennart section of Robeson County before marrying Effie Harrell and moving to her homestead near Saddletree. He purchased her family's farm and spent years overseeing its operation. Tolar served as county commissioner from 1939 until 1962. He was known for his love of fishing and hunting. This staged photograph by a reporter from *The Robesonian* was taken after one of the hunts he hosted on his farm. (Courtesy Historic Robeson, Inc.)

Jack Bullard, a student of Rowland teacher C.E. Morrison, killed this 300-pound black bear outside of Rowland in the spring of 1952. (Courtesy C.E. Morrison Collection, McMurray McKellar Historical Museum, Rowland.)

Although not politically correct by today's standards, minstrel shows were a favorite source of entertainment in the late 19th and early 20th centuries. This show was held in the Red Springs Opera House, which now houses the B.C. Moore Department Store. (Courtesy McKay Family Photograph Collection, in the possession of S.C. Edgerton.)

The students and teachers of Ten Mile School entered this float in the Robeson County School contest on January 26, 1911. The women of the Ten Mile community worked long hours decorating the wagon. (Courtesy Kate Biggs Collection.)

This wonderful float of the Ashpole Coon Hunters Club is pulled down Main Street Fairmont by a truck advertising Lewis-Brady Builders Supply. (Courtesy Town of Fairmont.)

Fairmont is known as a town that knows how to host a parade. The annual Farmer's Day parade was held in early April. (Courtesy Town of Fairmont.)

This drawing of the Carolina Civic Center by Sam Pait was based on a photograph that appeared in the June 18, 1928 issue of *The Robesonian*. Built by the Lumberton Theater Company, comprised of Dr. R.S. Beam, Dr. E.L. Bowman, and K.M. Barnes, the theater served the county for decades before falling into disrepair. The city of Lumberton purchased the property in 1980 for the sum of $55,000 and a fund-raising campaign was begun to refurbish the theater. Fifty-seven years to the day of its opening the restored building was reopened to the public. (Courtesy Carolina Civic Center.)

The African American Cultural Center is located on West Third Street in Lumberton alongside the Lumber River. The center is operated by Hilda Hubbard and was established to maintain and house an African-American Hall of Fame and Resource Center. (Courtesy African American Cultural Center.)

Fairmont native Willis Spruill Jr. a notable violinist performed at the grand opening of the African-American Cultural Center in Lumberton. Spruill has gone on to attend the North Carolina School of the Arts. (Courtesy African American Cultural Center.)

The 1932 Rowland baseball team was the winner of the "Shoe Heel League," having won 44 of the 54 games they played. Red Johnson served as manager and catcher while Stuart Evans was business manager. Nate Andrews, "Hog" McCormick, and Ralph Brake were pitchers for the team. (Courtesy McMurray McKellar Historical Museum, Rowland.)

The 1916 Lumberton Baseball Team was pennant runners-up for the North Carolina Amateur championship. Pictured from left to right are Lee Stone, ? Hodgin, Ed Pope, ? Smith, Knox Proctor, Chief Person, ? Minle, Luke Barnes, Edgar Bundy, Chuck Galloway, Rob Love, Carl C. Edens, and Lee Correll. (Courtesy John and Betty Edens.)

The St. Pauls American Legion Auxiliary was organized in 1919 and soon after that time organized a children's auxiliary. Helen Seawell Sharpe, the first girl on the second row, remembers the group helping Misses Julia and Esther McNeill sell poppies on Memorial Day each year. Sharpe's sister, Joyce, is the second person in the first row. (Courtesy Helen Seawell Sharpe.)

This photograph of a group of Boy Scouts was taken aboard a Navy ship on August 7, 1947 at Jacksonville, Florida. Kneeling from left to right are B.H. Blake, D.H. Bryant, E.T. Williams, C.W. Townsend, and C.R. Scott. Standing are A.M. Sharpe-leader, W.C. Edmundson, Billy Mitchell, W.A. McMillan, and J.J. Scott. (Courtesy Historic Robeson, Inc.)

On December 1, 1952 the centennial of the incorporation of Lumberton was celebrated with a play performed at the high school auditorium. This photograph commemorates surveyor Jacobs Rhodes (portrayed by W.F. French), who holds his map, which divided the property of Gen. John Willis into lots. Also pictured are Leslie Huntley as Henry Lightfoot, Joe Hill Barrinton as William Tatum, Dick Prevatt as Col. William Moore, Pat Treadaway as Sheriff Samuel Bridgers, and Wilton Barnes as Col. Elias Barnes. (Courtesy Historic Robeson, Inc.)

On August 16, 1787 a lottery drawing was held for the Lumberton Lots. Seated at the desk is I. Murchison Biggs portraying Judge Col. John Blount; seated behind the box is Wesley C. Watts portraying Clerk of Court Josiah Barnes. Lubin Prevatte portrayed the young John L. McLean, who actually drew the lottery tickets. (Courtesy Historic Robeson, Inc.)

On October 18, 1939 the town of Rowland celebrated its proud 50-year heritage. Special guest Gov. Clyde Hoey is shown in the far left of the backseat; next to him is Mrs. May Rowland Shaw, daughter of Colonel Rowland for whom the town was named; and Mayor J.C. "Pete" Ward. Town clerk Leverne Adams is shown standing alongside the car. (Courtesy McMurray McKellar Historical Museum, Rowland.)

Robert Doares, Maxton native, spent years walking the streets of Maxton as a child. He moved to New York where he spent years as a free-lance book and magazine illustrator. He was inspired to create *Centennial Parade* when returning to Maxton on April 6, 1974 for the town's centennial celebration. The work not only records the events of the day but also serves as a reminder of the businesses, many of which no longer exist, that once lined the street. In the background, the Patterson Building, once home to the Bank of Robeson and now housing the town office, stands guard over the skyline as she has done since 1911. (Courtesy Maxton Historical Society.)

Hector MacLean, chairman of the Robeson County Bicentennial Commission, opens the year-long celebration of the county's bicentennial. MacLean greeted the crowd with "All of you are distinguished guests on this occasion. If you are from Robeson County, you a distinguished guest for that and no other reason." (Courtesy UNCP University Relations.)

A crowd of nearly 500 gathered in front of the courthouse on January 6, 1987 to hear the Honorable H.A. "Sandy" McKinnon, retired Superior Court Judge, present a brief history of the county. As we look at this bicentennial celebration let's look forward to the future, and know that we must spend every day saving the bits and pieces of our history. (Courtesy UNCP University Relations.)

Visit us at
arcadiapublishing.com

Printed in the USA
CPSIA information can be obtained
at www.ICGtesting.com
LVHW010025081123
763339LV00008B/24

9 781531 610319